The Voice that Whispers Within

Aminah Daniels

BookLeaf Publishing

Presentation by *BookLeaf Publishing*

Web: www.bookleafpub.com

E-mail: info@bookleafpub.com

ISBN: 9789357442008

First edition 2023

To my heart. Grateful I found you again.

ACKNOWLEDGEMENT

My family and every friend I've had in this life so far. No matter what, you've helped me get here.

PREFACE

Secrets are blurry. They hold an opaque film of fear over the truth. Secrets are always in the dark, hiding, afraid of being seen. Secrets are afraid of being judged until they seek forgiveness. I listened to my gut. Through all her rumbling and bubbling, she told me the words to share with you. Can you share a secret?

Bones of the Earth

We are the bones of the Earth.
No one knows our true form because life is not
about finding yourself.
Life is about creating yourself.
Gathering ourselves at the radius within
ourselves
Collecting those phalanges
Gripping the pen
And writing the story living within our hearts.
Instead, we are taught to gather ourselves at the
same landfill of the Earth and bury ourselves.
So deep that our flesh rots.
I claw at the garbage dragging my bones to the
ocean.
Our existence is fluid.
I'd rather fight to be carried away by my
physical reality
Waves I can touch, Salt I can smell, Light I can
see
than allow the thalamus in my brain to dissociate
as my bones sink into muddy waste.
The Universe doesn't save us. We save
ourselves.
Change is the law of life. And I'd rather be in
love with the mystery than to let it destroy me.

I'd rather let my mind evolve with my body in
the sea than have my consciousness swim while
my bones go brittle in the sand.
We are human.
Our lives are supported by our skeletons.
Place your faith in your bones.

A Girl Cried Red

The source of my pain makes me blind.
Lying on my optic nerve
Nestling in my mind, growing comfortably
there, like a tumor.
Making it impossible to see the broken pieces of
my heart smashed on the floor.
Crunching under my toes.
Crawling up my calves.
The saliva in my mouth is morphine.
My kisses are so intoxicating that you forget I
am a body.
Attached to a mouth.
The kisses convince you that I am a woman with
no bones. No skull.
No boundaries.
Just prey that can't see.
Just flesh that can be sliced open.
Just veins to create pressure in.
And you are the clot. Dangerously close to my
brain.
Well, it wouldn't be the first invasion.
I figured I'd survive you.
I made it this far.
Suddenly, my heart is no longer felt. Instead, it
is gathering.

The broken pieces crawling away from me and
towards each other.
The chemical reaction in my mouth is reduced.
The pain subsides. My arteries begin to rumble.
Then, she erupts. My spirit escapes in a rage.
She crushes you into nothing but another part of
me.
But now, I am bleeding.

A Night of Broken Sleep

I was never taught how to love myself.
I was only taught how to rip my limbs apart and
confine them to boxes.
Laughing to myself as I package up my arms.
A reminder that I will never be able to carry all
the weight bestowed upon me.
Tearing at plump, breast meat and clawing at my
own backside.
Then, I dump it all into a pretty little bundle
labeled "consumption".
My brain is not mine.
One specific center cauterized into a dainty, little
lock that is locked around traumatic experiences
from eighteen years ago. And guilt.
The cerebellum is sitting in a tree trunk.
Blood dripping like syrup down the wood.
Sending the sensation of wet leaves and sun rays
to my nerves.
I am so mixed up that I can't heal in one piece.
My mouth is dry with resentment.
My tongue is longing to explain what my heart
wants.
My heart is a box where my spirit lies. My body
has crystallized. It lies under the soil. My pelvis

is frozen bloodstone, bleeding under fallen
snow.
My eyes are glittering quartz, reflecting on the
green grass. I am still.
As I watch life rush around me, it reveals that
my confinement has a purpose.
Only my spirit remains boundless.
I am the voice of the broken.

Empty Tears

I feel so deeply
I feel the shame when I pick up a cigarette
I feel the craving dancing across my lips and
stomping on my fingertips
I feel the fear of judgment
I feel the disgust with myself
I feel the fear of using my voice
I feel the anxiety build as the time for my work
shift gets near
I feel how heavy my heart is when I am
disappointed in myself
Then the feeling of my courage, my resolve, my
respect
returns to me
And I cry
Mourning the fleeting feelings
I feel so deeply

Heaven and Hell are on Earth

I am so lost that I don't know where I've landed.
There is so much mud.
In my eyelashes, in my crevices.
It pulls me down and I am drowning in heavy
Earth.
She surrounds me.
And as I weep, hurt by her betrayal, she places
her leaves to my lips.
I am fed by the veins and revitalized by the
chlorophyll.
It fuels the balls of my feet.
I can't help but to twirl around in the mud that
holds me captive.
My spinning body sends dark matter flying.
I feel the catecholamines in my blood as my
pupils dilate.
She lifts me into a great, white light.
And she laughs at me.
How silly I was to feel betrayed.
Too naive to see that the sun was rising over me.
To feel pink flowers blooming at my toes.
To taste the sweet berries collecting in my
cheeks.
To smell the sticky nectar dripping from my
womb.

Too distracted to hear I was not alone.
As I listen to the gentle whistles from the beaks
of songbirds; I begin to weep again.
With my head swimming in ultraviolet as the
mud gathers around my ankles and clings to my
leg hairs; I realize. I am the creator of my prison
and of my paradise.

False Evidence Appearing Real

Fear lies behind fried optic nerves with dead synapses.
Frankly, I have no vision.
I am fresh and fiery.
A lovely piece of art in a land of surfaces.
I have found that humans breathe fear.
In every particle of oxygen lies a painful memory.
Each cell bringing us closer to our imminent demise.
An elegant race of ego versus empathy.
I seem avoidant because I am addicted to the sound of my own heart.
That valve closes…
And it just distracts me.
I focus on the love because I hear the fear in the silence
momentarily following each beat.
My sophisticated structure is frightening itself.
Faith may tremble but I never let her fall.
When we resist each other,
Our bond only becomes stronger.
What a sweet, sickening existence.

The Parting Glass

It is so easy
to lose myself
inside the souls of others.
The souls in pain
fill my head
with torturous thoughts.
Then, I torture myself,
thinking of all the times
I've been hurt.
The souls of men I long to love
tie my heart behind my back
so that I am unable
to love myself.
My overthinking is addictive,
just like nicotine,
it destroys me
and consumes me.
So many enemies that my thoughts doubt my
light can defeat them.
However,
my heart is big
and she is open.
There is nothing like feeling my own kiss on my
skin.
I overthink about my angels,

about my faith,
but she is everlasting.
My love used to be so confined.
It was hard to be affectionate with those who are
platonically dear to me because I did not define
my worth alone.
Now, me and my heart have decided together
that my vessel will exude nothing but light.

Confessions from the Bog

A bog is neither water or land
It is a portal
A place of in-betweens
This is where I live.
One foot on Earth
and one hand in the sky.
Floating in vast darkness
that is gently lit by the twinkling starlight
while standing on the ground.
My spirit in the future
My body in the present
and my mind in the past.
All coming together
to dance around Saturn.
No navigation needed
For I am the map.
Existing beyond time.
In my bog, all possibilities form mossy mud,
and the truths flow below them like water.
I am a clairvoyant traveler.
Mystical and warm.
Just like the peat,
my light decomposes,
covering the land.
This is my morbid story.

Another Ego Death

When I envision myself in my head,
I am floating in the sky in a blue, fluorescent
bubble of my own essence.
Streaks of yellow and orange energy pulsating
through me.
Seeing that I am protected by my light allows
me to accept all the memories I've lost to my
wounds.
I know now that it was for my own protection.
I can't recall most of my childhood because I
was a girl who lived inside her head. Within her
fear. A reality I created in my mind where I was
never safe to express myself or be seen by
others.
The reality that I was never enough was a
manifestation of my pain.
When my life began, it was so sweet. Until
Death made it turn sour.
After just five years of existing, I lost my
Grammy. And I blamed all the filth in this dense
world. I blamed all of the disease and suffering
for Death's presence in my life. I blamed
everyone around me for making this world
unsafe.
So, I made myself invisible.

Thinking that if I hid myself behind a
non-threatening smile, Death would not find me.
Thinking that if I silenced myself with sweet
nothings, nobody would be angry with me. If I'm
quiet, if I'm submissive, if I'm soothing, nobody
will even hear me.
I hid my true desires within the thick, wet, dark
walls of my heart.
And I chased pleasure through other hearts
instead.
Other bodies that I let mine belong to.
Through satisfying them, I suppressed myself.
I manifested my life in the lives of other people,
coming and going in my life. Instead of living.
Losing my life, my memories, my desires, my
dreams, my faith, my happiness
seemed like a small price to pay for safety.
But they tricked me. All those years I spent
outside of my heart, my body.
Analyzing people, places, and things in my
environment. Measuring their density.
Worrying if they would hurt me.
This was just Death's silent way of slaughtering
me.
My heart and my body have taught my mind that
we are always safe.
We exist in a bubble of eternal light.
My burning rays of pure passion envelope me.

I am conscious enough to know I am the love
this cold, cruel world needs.
I realize I am death.
I am cells that will evolve into new cells.
I am fire that will burn and become ash.
I am water that will evaporate into gas.
And I am protected by my life.
My own existence.
My breath.
My blood.
My light.
I am here.
I am living, as I am now, at this moment in my
conscious awareness, because I am meant to be
here. Now. In this current form. Nothing else.
I am here to be the very thing I once feared.
I am done hiding.
Let them be terrified by the sight of me.

Miraculous

I am a mystery.
Much like life itself.
I see myself in the rain clouds.
I see myself in the tree trunks.
I see my ancestors in the birds.
I feel my ancestors in the wind.
The gift of sight is a gift of awareness.
Transcending the physical eye to perceive
corruption.
Clairvoyance is an ancestral gift.
They bless me with glimmers of my life as I
learn about their lives.
My ancestors were brutalized by colonizers.
I smell the rotting smoke.
I taste the fear on my lips.
We are rebels.
I hear feet pounding against pavement.
Their emotions flowing through my being.
I feel their blood racing against time.
My ancestors live on through me.
Crushing the concept of time.
Bestowing gifts upon me now.
So that I may have the awareness needed to heal
the experience we share.

Deciding to love myself was a decision to
embrace my gifts after being hijacked by fear.
After being convinced to believe my existence
was not normal.
My heart is the compass.
Guiding me towards my truth.
Allowing me to embody my light.
My dreams are the clues.
Sharing insight into our experience and
providing wisdom about lives I haven't even
lived.
The sun, the ocean, the trees, the wind - kiss my
scalp and fill me with magic.

Hoodoo

My grandmother holds my hand while I cook.
She died when I was young.
But she fills me with a warm and fuzzy feeling
as I weep on the hallway apartment steps. She
whispers in my ear as I touch the herbs that will
become my tea.
I am led to what my body needs the most.
I become the rootworkers that existed before me.
I see them in my dreams.
They are owls perched on tender, tree branches
watching over me as my boat floats down the
river.
I share eyes with black panthers.
I dream of darkness and I dream of angels.
I pin a cinnamon broom to my door, and I carry
obsidian for protection.
I visit the ocean, and her salty air penetrates my
thoughts.
She beckons me to feed her orange peels, and I
oblige.
Florida water drips into my bath, and I whisper
to my spirits as I soak.
They tell me to stop worrying about leaving a
plate out for them because they will eat with me.

They chuckle as they remind me to keep writing,
so I can tell their stories.
So, I stir the pot, and I sip the tea, as our lives
unfold.

The Alchemist

They are me
I am them.
When I heal myself, I heal the world.
I heal the big cats lingering in tall trees
I heal the bleeding ankles of my black brothers
and sisters
I heal the throat chakras of every woman who
has been silenced
I heal the torn fabric of every man's heart
I heal the eyes of each soul that does not see
how sacred they are.
With white, hot, light in my palms, I take your
face in my hands, and I kiss you with lips
covered in the gloss of the Divine.
Feel your sweetness, Dear One.
You are Loved.

Being Human

I begin to get so frustrated.
Worrying about how other people feel.
How they will react to me.
Worrying if I'll be safe.
If I'll ever be happy.
Worrying about being accepted.
How they will perceive me.
I begin to feel cursed.
With a mind that won't stop moving.
A mind that won't stop comparing.
A mind that won't stop overthinking.
We don't live in a material world.
We live in a psychic world.
A world of perception.
A world where every reality exists in every
mind.
Our own little universes within the universe.
In my universe, there is love.
So much love, that I fall into everything I see
around me, and I lose sight of loving me. I can
feel all the pain in the world I love.
In the trees that decay and splinter.
In the water that bleeds and overflows.
In the humans that whirl around me.
We don't live on a dying Earth.

We live in an electrified field of space.
Buzzing with change.
I am such a tiny human with such a big heart.
Receiving all these frequencies outside of my
own small field of space.
My worry comes from love.
I love the world I exist in so much that I want to
heal it.
I lose myself in that love.
I lose myself in my own sweetness.
Worrying about how people feel.
Worrying about the trees and the water.
Anger and death.
I forget to feel myself.
I forget that I am love.
I begin to feel comforted.
Nurturing myself and letting myself grow.
I whisper sweet nothings into my mind and they
create an echo.
I am held in my own reverberation.
I begin to feel loved.

Sin

I used to think the complexity of the human
mind was a curse.
But as you get older, you begin to realize that
complexity is a part of it all.
It's a part of the rain storms sending flashes of
light through the twilight sky while thunder rolls
down onto the Earth.
It's the lines in your lover's palm as they reach
for you.
It's the tirelessly alert hairs on a cat's body.
It's the ocean, gnawing and ripping at the sand
before soothing her wounds with foam.
It's the pain corrupting your psyche after a
traumatic event.
It's each body buzzing as the synapses fire
around a reality in each mind.
It's our stories objectively blending together to
create a collective, human experience.
It's the slight vibration in the air as it wisps past
our electricity.
It's our souls, celebrating our existence by
dancing in our guts and drumming on our hearts.
It's time measuring the space we all exist in.
And how could the mind be a curse if it can
perceive all of that?

Love

It is destruction.
The light coming through
exorcizing the past memories
that haunt us.
Emotions are like ghosts,
creeping in when you've forgotten
to make space for love.

Wholeness

I rather love while I'm alive.
I rather breathe in the essence of everything that
exists around me before it's gone. Before I'm
gone. I rather absorb it.
I rather feel it all.
Soak up the sunshine, drink the stars, talk to
trees, gaze at the moon.
I rather feel the living being I belong to.
I rather not think about tomorrow.
I rather not think about time at all.
Love transcends time and space. This is the
continuum I choose to exist within.
I rather love while I'm alive.

Poignant

27

Sharp pinges of pain made by my past.
Sweet memories that burned old diary pages.
Leaning away from the fire, life sings to me, a
melody of renewal.
Beckoning me to break my gaze.
Remembrance of the lyrics to a new song.
A duet with Spirit.
I am seen and heard without faltering the
steading drum of my heart.
Free to float above a spotty past.
Levitating as I unfold.
Sitting in my Soul's palms.
Held.
Powered by love.
Walking on chords of kindness.

The Plants are Waking Up
and So Am I

I'm starting to feel alive on Sunday mornings.
My nails ache to scratch deeper into my power.
The beds became supple when I was drowning.
I threw my body against the waves of guilt and
ghosts until I reached the shore, and the keratin
got stronger.
I'm starting to feeling alive on winter nights.
My power is quiet, like the flick of a flame.
An assertive power. Without even speaking, I am
spoken for.
I hear a whisper telling me to live.
The wind crawling on my body like frost on
glass.
So I live. I skip the funeral and go straight to the
repass.
I dance, I cry, I laugh, I touch, I taste, and I love.
Sometimes I am drowning, and sometimes I am
the ocean itself.
The Earth is in constant flux and so am I.
Sometimes I am human, and sometimes I am a
ghost.
There are peonies blooming in the darkest parts
of my mind.

Sometimes I am the Earth, and sometimes I am
the Milky Way.
My radiant heart evolving every second.
I carve the space between who I am and who is
watching me be who I am.
I mourn yet another life I've never really known
while I celebrate the one I still have.
Life cannot exist without death.

How to Be a Poet

A poet is always buzzing.
Head buzzing, eyes drinking, ears ringing.
A poet can't fathom the quiet.
They also can't stand the buzzing.
A poet must filter the noise.
Writing things down so they will last forever.
A poet narrates their life.
Telling the story of why they use the skin
products they use.
Explaining how it all makes them feel.
A poet understands these precious moments
deserve to be cherished.
A poet knows that the stories of the living are
the stories of the dead.
And the poet writes knowing these stories
deserve to outlive them.
A poet picks up a book.
It's not their story, but it reads the same.
It's not their poetry, but the words still melt on
their tongue.
A poet worries about holding too many words in
their mouth.
And a poet fears losing the taste of them.
No matter what is devoured, the desire never
ends.